Cricket

Clive Gifford

W
FRANKLIN WATTS
LONDON•SYDNEY

Franklin Watts

First published in Great Britain in 2016 by The Watts Publishing Group

Copyright © The Watts Publishing Group, 2016

Editors: Katie Dicker & Gerard Cheshire
Art direction: Rahul Dhiman (Q2AMedia)
Designer: Rohit Juneja, Cheena Yadav (Q2AMedia)
Picture researcher: Nivisha Sinha (Q2AMedia)

Picture credits:
t=top b=bottom c=centre l=left r=right

Front Cover: Aijaz Rahi/AP Photo.
Back Cover: Ross Setford/AP Photo, Aijaz Rahi/ AP Photo, Dave Thompson/AP Photo, Mark J. Terrill/AP Photo, Jay LaPrete/AP Photo, Anja Niedringhaus/AP Photo.
Title Page: Carl Fourie/AP Photo.
Imprint Page: Lee Smith/LV Championship.
Insides: Karel Prinsloo/AP Photo: 4, Themba Hadebe/AP Photo: 5, Sandra Mu/Getty Images: 6, Ajit Solanki/AP Photo: 7, Lee Smith/LV Championship: 8, Richard Heathcote/Getty Images: 9, Darren England/Newspix/Rex Features: 10, Tertius Pickard/Gallo Images/Getty Images: 11, Bikas Das/AP Photo: 12, Obed Zilwa/AP Photo: 13, Ross Setford/AP Photo: 14l, Corey Davis, Pool/AP Photo: 14r, Rick Rycroft/AP Photo: 15, Aijaz Rahi/ AP Photo: 16, Carl Fourie/AP Photo: 17, Aman Sharma/AP Photo: 18, Aman Sharma/AP Photo: 19, Tom Hevezi/AP Photo: 20, Jon Super/AP Photo: 21, Rob Griffith/AP Photo: 22, Tom Hevezi/AP Photo: 23, Jack Dawes/Daily Mail/Rex Features: 24, AP Photo: 25, Quinn Rooney/Getty Images: 26, Alastair Grant/AP Photo: 27, AP Photo: 28.

ISBN: 978 1 4451 4962 2

Note: At the time of going to press, the statistics in this book were up to date. However, due to the nature of sport, it is possible that some of these may now be out of date.

Printed in China

Franklin Watts
An imprint of
Hachette Children's Group
Part of The Watts Publishing Group
Carmelite House
50 Victoria Embankment
London EC4Y 0DZ

An Hachette UK Company
www.hachette.co.uk

www.franklinwatts.co.uk

MIX
Paper from responsible sources
FSC® C104740
www.fsc.org

Contents

Batting and bowling 4

First-class cricket 6

The County Championship..................................... 8

The Sheffield Shield and Sunfoil Series 10

One-day internationals 12

The Cricket World Cup.. 14

The World Twenty20 16

The Indian Premier League 18

Test match cricket.. 20

The Ashes... 22

Great players and teams 24

Women's cricket... 26

Timeline and winner tables.................................... 28

Glossary and further info...................................... 30

Index... 32

*Words in **bold** are in the glossary on page 30

Batting and bowling

Cricket is a bat-and-ball sport with 11 players in each team. One team bats with two players at a time, each trying to score **runs**. The other team fields and bowls the ball, with six bowls making up each **over**. The fielding team tries to get the opposing batsmen called 'out', and also tries to stop them from scoring runs. The team that scores the most runs wins.

They're out!

Each batsman plays until he is called out (also known as losing their **wicket**). This can occur in a number of ways, including being bowled (when the ball bowled by the bowler hits the **stumps**), caught (when a fielder catches the ball hit by the batsman before it hits the ground) or run out (when a fielder throws the ball to hit the stumps whilst the batsman is out of his **batting crease**). Once out, a player is replaced by another batsman from their team. When ten players are out, the team's **innings** is over. In **limited overs** games (see page 12), a team also finishes their innings once they have faced their set number of overs.

Pakistan batsman Kamran Akmal prepares to play a shot as he stands in front of his stumps.

Reaching the boundary

The edge of a cricket ground is called the **boundary** and is usually marked by a rope. A strike of the ball that reaches the boundary scores four runs (a 'four') if it bounces on the ground beforehand, or six runs (a 'six') if it passes the boundary still airborne.

Fit and focused

Although cricket can be seen as slow-paced compared to some sports, it is not a gentle game. Top players have to be fit and focused. When batting, they wear plenty of protective clothing as the fastest bowlers can bowl at speeds approaching 140kph (90mph). The **wicket-keeper**, who fields the ball behind the stumps, is often protected with leg pads, body padding and a helmet.

In competition

World cricket is organised by the International Cricket Council (ICC). Many different competitions exist for men's cricket, women's cricket and youth team cricket all over the world.

GREAT SPORTING STATS

Catches often win matches and a team's wicket-keeper is in the best position to take a catch. On his retirement in 2012, South African wicket-keeper Mark Boucher had taken 532 catches in **Test matches** – a record.

Mark Boucher's skill as a wicket-keeper helped the South African team to many victories.

First-class cricket

First-class cricket is the highest level of cricket played by clubs, regions or other teams in a country. First-class cricket matches are usually held over three or four days of action and feature two batting innings for each side.

National competitions

Every major cricketing nation has a first-class competition, from the County Championship in Britain (see pages 8–9) to the Quaid-i-Azam Trophy in Pakistan. In the West Indies, the regional four-day competition has sometimes invited an overseas team, such as England A or the Kenyan national cricket team, to take part.

Plunket Shield

New Zealand's first-class championship is one of the longest-running cricket competitions. It was first held in 1906. It has been known by many names, but is currently called the Plunket Shield and runs from November to April. The four-day games are intense and long. There are more than 120 overs and over six hours play each day. Of the six competing teams, the Otago Volts have been the unluckiest and have not won the competition in the past 12 seasons.

Hamish Bennett bowls a delivery during the final day of the Plunket Shield match between the Canterbury Wizards and the Northern Knights.

The Ranji Trophy

The Cricket Championship of India, now known as the Ranji Trophy, began in 1934. It features a two-tier system, with 18 teams in tier one (divided equally into Group A and Group B), and nine teams in tier two (Group C). After a series of **round robin** games, the top two teams from Group C join the top three teams from Group A and B for a knockout competition. The 2012/13 winners, Mumbai, are also the competition's most successful side with a staggering 40 trophies.

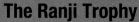

GREAT SPORTING STATS

The three highest individual batting scores of all time have been in first-class competitions in England, Pakistan and Australia. These are: 501 not out — Brian Lara playing for Warwickshire v Durham, 1994; 499 — Hanif Mohammad playing for Karachi v Bahawalpur, 1959; 452 not out — Donald Bradman playing for New South Wales v Queensland, 1930.

Vikram Solanki, playing for Rajasthan in the Ranji Trophy, strikes the ball while the Gujarat wicket-keeper looks on.

The County Championship

The County Championship, held in England and Wales, is the longest-running first-class competition in the world. It was first held in 1890, with eight sides representing English counties. It now includes 18 county teams, including one based in Wales (Glamorgan) and its newest recruit, Durham, which joined in 1992.

Marcus Trescothick, playing for Somerset, hits a four during a County Championship game.

Busy season

The County Championship season starts in April and ends in September. All teams play a hectic schedule of 16 four-day matches, fitted in between other competitions. Most teams feature at least one overseas player. In 2015, South Africa's Ashwell Prince made the most County Championship runs (1,478) of all batsmen while playing for Lancashire.

County grounds

Each county team has one or more home grounds where they play eight matches. Some, such as Lords (used by Middlesex), Edgbaston (Warwickshire) or Old Trafford (Lancashire) are also famous venues internationally. Some grounds have a reputation for having particularly good conditions for batting or bowling. In 2007, Somerset's county ground, at Taunton, saw two of the top seven highest scores of all time, including 850 runs for seven batsmen (850–7) **declared** by the home team.

21st century changes

In 2000, the County Championship teams were divided into two divisions of nine teams each. At the end of each season, one team is **relegated** and another is **promoted** between the divisions, adding extra tension in matches. No county is safe. In 2011, Lancashire won the County Championship, but was relegated from the top division just a year later.

Points scoring

Sixteen points are awarded for a win and five points for a draw. In addition, there are bonus points for good batting or bowling. Yorkshire won back-to-back championships in 2014 and 2015, the latter by a comfortable 68 points. In contrast, Nottinghamshire and Somerset topped the table, both with 214 points, in 2010. Nottinghamshire were crowned champions as they had won more games overall.

Bonus points are gained in the first 110 overs of a team's first innings. The current bonus points are:

Batting
200–249 runs = 1 point
250–299 runs = 2 points
300–349 runs = 3 points
350–399 runs = 4 points

Bowling
3–5 wickets: 1 point
6–8 wickets: 2 points
9–10 wickets: 3 points

Nottinghamshire celebrate winning the County Championship in 2010 after they took a third Lancashire wicket and gained the crucial bonus point to make them champions.

The Sheffield Shield and Sunfoil Series

Both South Africa and Australia have similar competitions to the UK's County Championship. The Sheffield Shield, in Australia, and the Sunfoil **Series**, in South Africa, are both held over four days, with each team playing two innings.

The Sheffield Shield

The Sheffield Shield (known as the Pura Cup between 1999 and 2009) is Australia's leading first-class cricket competition. The six states of Queensland, Tasmania, New South Wales, Victoria, South Australia and Western Australia play each other twice over the season. The top two sides face each other in a final match held at the home ground of the team that currently leads the league.

The Sunfoil Series

South Africa's leading competition began in 1889 with just two teams – Kimberley and Transvaal. For a century, it was known as the Currie Cup before becoming the Castle Cup (from 1990), the SuperSport Series (from 1996) and the Sunfoil Series (from 2012). Since 2005, the competition has featured six regional teams playing each other home and away in a ten-match season.

Shane Watson bowls during a Sheffield Shield match between the Queensland Bulls and the South Australia Redbacks.

Playing for points

In the Sunfoil Series, ten points go to a team for winning a match. Teams batting in their first innings score a bonus point when they reach 150 runs, with a further 0.02 bonus points added for every run above that. This means that should a team make 300 runs in their first innings, they would receive a total of four bonus points. In the 2014/15 series, the Highveld Lions won for the first time in 15 years, ending the dominance of the Titans and Cobras who had won during the previous six seasons.

JP Duminy plays an attractive attacking shot for his team, the Nashua Cape Cobras, against the Highveld Lions.

GREAT SPORTING STATS

The three leading runs-scorers in the history of the Sunfoil Series competition are Graeme Pollock (12,409 runs), Peter Kirsten (11,835 runs) and Jimmy Cook (11,307 runs). In October 2009, Jimmy Cook's son, Stephen, scored a competition record of 390 runs in an innings, which included 53 fours.

One-day internationals

One-day internationals (**ODIs**) are limited overs matches between two national teams. There have been over 3,000 ODIs since the very first match was played in 1971 as a way of pleasing spectators after rain had washed out an Australia v England Test match (see pages 20–21). ODIs usually offer a definite result in just a single day's play.

Limited overs games

Limited overs games see each team bat for a set amount of overs, provided they still have batsmen in the game. Limited overs competitions within countries (for clubs or counties) are usually 40 overs per side. One-day internationals are now always 50 overs per side.

Bowling and fielding

The bowling team looks to stifle runs and get the opposition team out. Each bowler is allowed to bowl a maximum of ten overs. Most ODI sides contain a number of **all-rounders** who can bowl some overs, but are also good batsmen. Every run is crucial, so fielders need to be athletic to dive and stop shots wherever possible.

Sachin Tendulkar is the all-time leading scorer in ODIs. On his retirement in 2012, he had scored 18,426 runs in ODIs.

South Africa's Makhaya Ntini is congratulated by teammates after taking a wicket during an ODI match against Australia. He ended with match-winning figures of six wickets for just 22 runs.

GREAT SPORTING STATS

In 2006, there were three mammoth scoring feats in ODIs. Australia racked up 434 runs in an ODI against South Africa, only to find themselves beaten as South Africa reached 438. Amazingly, three months later that score was beaten by Sri Lanka scoring 443-9 against the Netherlands — an all-time record in ODIs.

Powerplays

For 20 of the 50 overs, the bowling team have to operate under what is called a powerplay. This sees them forced to place many fielders close to the batsmen, leaving large parts of the pitch free for potential run-scoring shots. Powerplay gives the batting team a temporary advantage, and adds extra excitement to a match.

ODI series and competitions

ODIs are often scheduled as part of a touring team's matches, meaning that a series of ODIs is normally played before or after a **Test match** series. Sometimes, a third team is invited to create a triangular tournament. In addition, there are ODI competitions such as the Cricket World Cup (see pages 14–15) and the ICC Champions Trophy, which is held every two years.

The Cricket World Cup

The ultimate ODI competition began in 1975, when England hosted a one-day international tournament of eight teams that was won by the West Indies. The ICC Cricket World Cup, as it is now known, is held once every four years and attracts major attention. For example, the 2015 tournament, in Australia and New Zealand, was televised in over 200 countries.

The ICC Cricket World Cup trophy

Pakistan captain, Imran Khan, celebrates as he takes the last English wicket to win Pakistan's first Cricket World Cup in 1992.

World Cup format

All ten of the leading cricket nations (those that have been granted Test match status, see pages 20-21) usually receive an invitation to the tournament. A further four places are available to teams that perform well in the ICC World Cup qualifying leagues and tournaments. For the 2015 World Cup, Ireland, Afghanistan, Scotland and UAE played well enough to qualify. All of the countries that play take part in a series of group games, which lead to **quarter-finals**, **semi-finals** and then a final.

Shock results

Recent tournaments have seen some exciting shock results, such as Ireland beating the West Indies in the group stage of the 2015 World Cup. In 2007, Ireland beat a strong Pakistan side in the group stage by bowling them out for just 132 runs, whilst Bangladesh surprisingly beat India in the group stage by bowling them all out for 191.

Mitchell Starc of Australia bowls during the 2015 ICC Cricket World Cup final match between Australia and New Zealand in Melbourne, Australia in 2015.

Best batting

Held in Australia and New Zealand, the 2015 World Cup saw a feast of exciting batting. New Zealand's Martin Guptill took the record for the highest individual score in World Cup history (237 not out), whilst his teammate Brendon McCullum recorded the fastest 50 runs in the tournament's history (51 runs off 18 balls). Yet the player voted man of the tournament was bowler Mitchell Starc, who took 22 wickets, helping to guide Australia towards their fifth World Cup victory.

The World Twenty20

An exciting new form of cricket began in 2003 and has since boomed in popularity. **Twenty20** cricket is a short, explosive, limited overs contest, with each team batting for 20 overs. Within four years it had its own international competition called the 'World Twenty20', featuring all the world's leading cricket nations.

Twenty20 tournaments

The first World Twenty20 was held in South Africa in 2007, and the tournament is generally held every two years. Since 2014, the tournament has featured 16 teams – all the Test match-playing nations, plus six qualifiers, which in the past have included Scotland, Ireland, Kenya and the Netherlands. In 2014, three new teams made their debut at the tournament – Nepal, Hong Kong and UAE.

England cricketer Craig Kieswetter hits a powerful shot during the final of the 2010 World Twenty20 between England and Australia.

Batting feats

Explosive batting and getting a high **run-rate** are crucial to success. Sri Lanka produced the tournament's highest score, with 260 from 120 balls, against Kenya in 2007. Two Sri Lankans are also in the top three run scorers of the competition's history. The top run scorer in a single series is India's Virat Kohli who scored 319 runs in the 2014 tournament.

Super Tens onwards

In the Group stage, the six qualifying teams join the two lowest-ranked Test teams and are split into two groups of four teams. The winner of each group goes through to join the Test teams (who skipped the Group stage) in the Super Ten stage. There, two groups of five teams play each other and the top two sides from each group play semi-finals to produce the finalists.

Bowling prowess

Although Twenty20 matches are all about runs, a brilliant bowling or fielding performance can also turn a game. In 2012, Sri Lankan bowler Ajantha Mendis took six wickets for just eight runs in the tournament's opening match against Zimbabwe. His team went on to earn themselves a place in the final.

In the 2014 World Twenty20, India's Virat Kohli averaged 106.33 runs each time he batted, an incredible feat. The highest individual score at the World Twenty20 in a single match was by Brendon McCullum, captain of the New Zealand side. He scored a staggering 123 runs from just 58 balls against Bangladesh in 2012.

Pakistan cricketer Imran Nazir is bowled out by Sri Lanka bowler Ajantha Mendis during the 2012 World Twenty20 semi-final. Mendis took 15 wickets in the tournament – more than any other bowler.

The Indian Premier League

Founded in 2007, the Indian Premier League (IPL) is a Twenty20 competition held in India during the spring. With thrilling cricket and showbusiness glamour, the tournament attracts a large television audience that enjoys watching Indian stars play with some of the finest overseas players in the game.

Tournament teams

When the IPL was formed, individuals and business groups bid for the right to own one of the eight founding teams (expanded to ten in 2011). Each squad now plays five other teams (selected at random) twice in a home-away format, and four other teams once. At the end of the season, the top four teams take part in a four-game **playoff** to determine the winner.

Players for sale

Unique to the IPL is its auction system, with the different teams bidding to buy the world's best players. In the IPL's first season, Indian captain Mahendra Singh Dhoni was the most expensive player at US$1.5 million (£1.04 million), a figure topped by the US$2.57 million (£1.75 million) paid for Indian cricketer Yuvraj Singh in 2015.

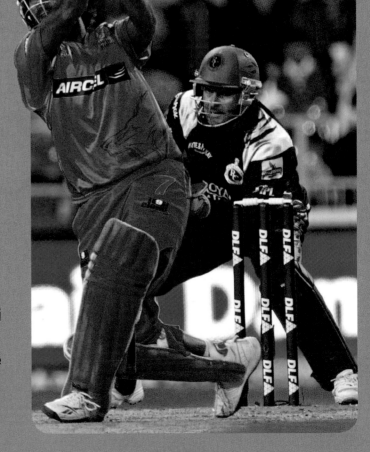

Mahendra Singh Dhoni in action (formerly the most expensive player at US$1.5 million). In 2010 and 2011, Dhoni captained the Chennai Super Kings to win the IPL.

Overseas players

The IPL regularly features talented overseas players from Australia, New Zealand, South Africa and the UK, among others. Australia's Shane Watson, for example, is the only IPL player to have won Man of the Series twice (in 2008 and 2013) and one of a few international cricketers to play for the same IPL team (the Rajasthan Royals) since the tournament began. In 2014, Australia's Glenn Maxwell won four Man of the Match awards as well as Man of the Series. In 2015, another Australian, David Warner, captained the Sunrisers Hyderabad, and ended the season as the tournament's leading run scorer (with 562 runs).

GREAT SPORTING STATS

Scoring is fast and furious in a typical IPL game, with scores of between 140–170 runs from just 20 overs. Yet in one 2013 IPL game, West Indies cricketer Chris Gayle of the Royal Challengers Bangalore hit an astonishing 175 runs from just 66 balls.

Shane Warne celebrates with other members of his Rajasthan Royals team during an IPL game against the Mumbai Indians.

Test match cricket

Test matches are the longest matches in the sport and are held between the top national cricket teams in the world. These five-day games offer the toughest possible challenge of a player's nerve and skill. They also test a team's ability to handle pressure and tough conditions to win matches.

England's Steven Finn bowling during the third Investec cricket Test match between England and South Africa at Lords Cricket Ground in 2012.

Test history

The first ever Test match took place in 1877, with Australia beating England by 45 runs. Since that time, over 2,000 Test matches have been played between the ten Test-playing nations, with Bangladesh becoming the latest Test team in 2000. Women's Test cricket began in 1934 and now also includes ten teams, with the Netherlands joining in 2007.

Five-day matches

A Test series consists of between two and six Test matches played in one country. Each Test match involves each team batting for two innings per side over five days' play, with usually about six hours of action each day. Every 80 overs, the fielding team is offered a new ball which is harder and bouncier than the old one.

Building an innings

Patience, stamina, nerve and skill are required to bat long, bowl hard and field skilfully throughout an entire Test match. Teams try to build big innings scores with their batsmen forming partnerships. If a side is struggling, they look to their last batsmen, known as **tailenders**, to stay in for a more established batsman at the other end to continue scoring runs, as well as scoring runs themselves.

Saving a game

Test matches can ebb and flow, with one team and then the other dominating. Bad weather can halt play and stop a team on top from achieving a win. As some matches near their end, a team may try to keep their wickets, so they are still batting at the end of the game. Even if a team has fewer runs, if they are still batting the game will end in a draw rather than a loss. This is called saving the game. In 2015, Bangladesh achieved this four times in five Test matches.

GREAT SPORTING STATS

If a team think they have scored enough runs in their innings and want to move the game on, they can **declare** the innings whilst they still have wickets left. In 1997, Sri Lanka had scored 952 for six wickets; they declared against India to win the game. In 2013, Australia declared their first innings at 237 for nine against India. A double-century score from Cheteshwar Pujara, however, saw India go on to win the Test match by an innings and 135 runs!

Shafiul Islam (second left) is surrounded by his Bangladesh teammates after taking the wicket of England's Jonathan Trott during a Test match.

The Ashes

The oldest Test series of all is the epic contest between Australia and England, known as **the Ashes**. The competition gets its name from a tiny urn said to hold the remains of the **bails** burned to celebrate Australia's defeat of England in 1882.

Series details

The Ashes series takes place every two years, but with Australian and English summers occurring at different times of the year, there is either 1½ years or 2½ years between each series. The contest is usually held over five matches, although four-match, and six-match series have been held.

England and Australia battle it out during the 2013 Ashes at the Emirates Durham International Cricket Ground.

Test venues

Some of the most famous grounds in world cricket are used for Ashes series, such as the Melbourne Cricket Ground (MCG), the traditional home of Tests starting on Boxing Day. In England, Lords in London is traditionally the host of the first match of the series, although other grounds have taken this honour in recent years, such as Sophia Gardens in Cardiff, Wales (2009 and 2015).

Changing fortunes

Both teams have had periods of success and dominance but between 1989 and 2005, Australia retained the Ashes in every series. The 2005 Ashes was one of the most dramatic in history, going right to the very last day of the series before England ran out narrow winners at the Oval in London. England were thrashed 5-0 in Australia in 2006/07 and 2013/14, but regained or retained the Ashes in 2009, 2010-11, 2013 and 2015. This leaves the overall tally of 32 Ashes series to Australia, 32 to England and five drawn.

England's Andrew Flintoff celebrates after running out Australian captain Ricky Ponting in the fifth Ashes Test in 2009.

GREAT SPORTING STATS

The most wickets taken by one bowler in an Ashes match is an incredible 19 out of 20 balls by English spin bowler, Jim Laker in the 1956 Old Trafford Test. Overall, Australia's Shane Warne has taken the most wickets in Ashes matches (195) followed by fellow Australians Glenn McGrath (157), Hugh Trumble (141), Dennis Lillee (128) and England s Ian Botham (128).

The five batsmen who have scored the most runs in Ashes Test matches are: Donald Bradman (Australia) 5,028; Jack Hobbs (England) 3,636; Allan Border (Australia) 3,548; David Gower (England) 3,269 and Steve Waugh (Australia) 3,200.

Women's cricket

Women's cricket has a long history. The first women's cricket club was formed in Yorkshire, England, in 1897. The first female Test match was played in 1934 and in 1997 a women's County Championship was set up in England. At international level, teams play Test matches, Twenty20 games, ODIs and a Women's World Cup.

Test matches

There are currently ten teams that play women's Test cricket, with Ireland and the Netherlands joining leading cricket nations such as Australia, England and India in 2000 and 2007 respectively. Matches are mostly held over four days, which has led to many matches ending in a draw. Australia and England have so far contested 20 women's Ashes series, with Australia winning seven, England six, and seven series drawn.

Australia's opening batswoman, Melissa Bulow, is surrounded by close fielders from India during a Test match.

Limited overs matches

Many women's matches are one-day games, with teams or clubs competing within a country, or one-day internationals with teams playing 50 overs per side. One of the longest running series is the Rose Bowl series between Australia and New Zealand, which has been played every season since 1985. Twenty20 games are also proving popular in women's cricket, with the first World Twenty20, held in 2009, won by England.

The Women's World Cup

The Women's Cricket World Cup was first held in 1973, and the 2013 competition saw the eight leading women's teams play a total of 25 matches in India. Australia and the West Indies reached the final, where Australia won the competition for the sixth time. Australia's Megan Schutt excelled in the final to become the leading wicket taker of the whole tournament.

England's Claire Taylor hits out in the final of the 2009's Women's Twenty20 World Cup. Taylor has scored over 1,000 Test runs and over 4,100 ODI runs for England.

GREAT SPORTING STATS

Australia have the best record in women's ODIs, having won 218 of the 282 games they have played. Their leading player of recent years, Karen Rolton, scored a record 4,814 runs in ODIs and 1,002 Test runs before retiring in 2010.

1877 First Test cricket match between England and Australia.

1889 South Africa plays its first Test match.

1890 First County Championship season in England.

1909 International Cricket Council (ICC) formed.

1932 India becomes the sixth nation to play Test match cricket.

1934 First ever women's Test match is held between England and Australia.

1947 England's Denis Compton scores 3,816 runs, the most in a first-class cricket season.

1948 Australia's Sir Donald Bradman plays his last Test match, against England, before retiring.

1952 Pakistan plays its first Test match, against India.

1955 New Zealand records the lowest ever Test match innings, all out for 26.

1968 Sir Garfield Sobers of the West Indies scores six sixes in a single over for the first time in a first-class cricket match.

1973 First Women's World Cup takes place.

1975 West Indies wins the first ever one-day international World Cup, beating Australia in the final.

1982 Sri Lanka becomes the first new Test playing nation in 30 years.

1992 Durham becomes the first new team in the English County Championship for over 70 years.

1994 Brian Lara, batting for Warwickshire, makes the highest ever first-class cricket score of 501 not out.

1997 Highest ever Test match score, 952 runs for 6 by Sri Lanka versus India.

2000 Bangladesh becomes the newest Test playing nation.

2003 First ever Twenty20 competition, the Twenty20 Cup, takes place in England and is won by Surrey.

2005 England win their first Ashes series against Australia since 1986/87.

2007 First ever World Twenty20 held in South Africa and is won by India.

2008 Indian Premier League (IPL) holds its first tournament. Rajasthan Royals win.

2008 India's Sachin Tendulkar passes Brian Lara's world record of 11,953 Test match runs.

2011 Tenth ICC World Cup is hosted by India, Sri Lanka and Bangladesh.

2015 Eleventh ICC World Cup is hosted by Australia and New Zealand.

Australia's Donald Bradman (1908–2001) is regarded as the greatest batsman of all time.

Winner tables

ICC Test Championship (correct 2015)

Team	Matches	Rating
South Africa	29	114
India	32	110
Australia	36	109
Pakistan	28	106
England	40	99
New Zealand	33	95
Sri Lanka	32	93
West Indies	29	76
Bangladesh	22	47

Cricket World Cup

Year	Winners	Runners-up
1983	India	West Indies
1987	Australia	England
1992	Pakistan	England
1996	Sri Lanka	Australia
1999	Australia	Pakistan
2003	Australia	India
2007	Australia	Sri Lanka
2011	India	Sri Lanka
2015	Australia	New Zealand

World Twenty20

Year	Hosts	Winners	Runners-up
2010	West Indies	England	Australia
2012	Sri Lanka	West Indies	Sri Lanka
2014	Bangladesh	Sri Lanka	India

Women's World Cup Winners

Year	Winners
1978	Australia
1982	Australia
1988	Australia
1993	England
1997	Australia
2000	New Zealand
2005	Australia
2009	England
2013	Australia

Recent Men's Ashes Winners

Year	Winners
1998–99	Australia
2001	England
2002–03	Australia
2005	England
2006–07	Australia
2009	England
2010–11	England
2013	England
2013–14	Australia
2015	England

Glossary and further info

All-rounder A player who is good at batting and either bowling or wicket-keeping.

Bails The small wooden cylinders placed horizontally on top of the stumps.

Batting crease The line running across a cricket pitch 1.22m in front of the stumps.

Boundary The edge of a cricket ground, usually marked by a rope. A struck ball which reaches this rope counts as four or six runs.

Century A score of 100 runs in cricket.

Declare When a team chooses to end their innings before they have lost all their wickets.

Innings The period when a batsman bats until he or she is out and lose their wicket. Can also mean an entire team's turn to bat.

Limited overs Matches where teams each have one batting innings lasting for a set number of overs.

ODI One-day international matches which are either 40 or 50 overs per side.

Over A series of six balls bowled by a bowler from one end of the pitch.

Playoff An extra match to decide the outcome of a competition; in IPL, four teams take part in a playoff to determine the winner.

Promoted Moved up a division of a league.

Quarter-finals Knockout matches for eight teams with the four winning sides entering the semi finals.

Relegated Dropped down to a lower division of a league.

Round robin A type of competition format where each team plays all the other teams in their group.

Run-rate The average number of runs scored per over.

Runs Points scored in cricket, most commonly by the batsman hitting the ball and running to the other end of the pitch.

Selectors The people who choose the players to form a cricket team.

Semi-finals A pair of matches with the winners of each match reaching the final of a competition.

Series A number of events or matches that come one after the other.

Stumps The three wooden sticks placed upright in the ground to form a wicket.

Tailenders Players who bat near the end of an innings who tend not to be known as great batsmen.

Test match The longest and most testing form of cricket, played over five days between two national teams.

The Ashes The name given to the Test match series between Australia and England held every two years.

Twenty20 An exciting new form of cricket in which each team bats for 20 overs.

Wicket A set of three upright sticks with two small sticks on top of them at which a cricket ball is bowled. Also used to describe the area of grass between the two wickets on a cricket pitch, and what a batsman has lost when he is out.

Wicket-keeper The player who stands behind the stumps and fields the ball (should it pass the batsman) using gloves and leg pads.

Websites

http://www.icc-cricket.com
The official website of the International Cricket Council, the organisation that runs world cricket.

http://www.espncricinfo.com
An enormous website with fixtures, news, statistics and results on every cricket competition in the world.

http://www.cricket365.com
Another large and comprehensive cricket news website with details of cricket competitions all over the world.

http://www.cricket20.com
A website devoted to all Twenty20 cricket competitions, including details of international games and past and future World Twenty20s.

http://www.ecb.co.uk
The England and Wales Cricket Board's website has lots of information and links to cricket clubs all over the UK, and features on the national men's and women's teams.

http://www.lords.org
The official website of the cricket ground in London, UK.

http://www.cricket.com.au
The official website of Cricket Australia is packed with features and information on state, national and international cricket.

http://www.caribbeancricket.com
An independent website about cricket competitions in the Caribbean, as well as news and features on the West Indies team.

http://www.blackcaps.co.nz
The official website of New Zealand Cricket, with details of competitions inside New Zealand as well as news of the national team.

http://www.mcg.org.au
The official website of the historic Melbourne Cricket Ground, complete with features and a timeline of major events.

http://www.iplt20.com
The official website of the Indian Premier League, with all the latest news about player auctions, matches and leading performances.

http://www.bbc.co.uk/sport/cricket
The BBC's website keeps you up to date with cricket that is being played worldwide.

http://www.banglacricket.com
A popular website for fans of Bangladeshi cricket.

Further reading

Young Wisden: A New Fan's Guide to Cricket – Tim De Lisle (A&C Black Publishers Ltd, 2007)
An excellent book about the game of cricket and how it is played.

Generation Cricket: Global Cricket – Clive Gifford (Wayland, 2015)
Learn more about the drama, action and skill involved in playing cricket.

Index

all-rounders 12

batting 4–9, 11–13, 15–17, 20–21, 23, 25–26, 28
boundary 5
bowling 4–6, 8–10, 12–15, 17, 21, 23–24

County Championships 6, 8–10, 26, 28
cricket grounds
    Edgbaston 8
    Lords 8, 22
    Melbourne Cricket Ground 22
    Old Trafford 8, 23
    Sophia Gardens 22
    Taunton 8
Cricket World Cup 13–15, 29

fielding 4, 12–13, 17, 20–21, 26

ICC Champions Trophy 13
ICC Test Championship 25, 29
Indian Premier League (IPL) 18–19, 28
innings 4, 6, 9–11, 15, 20–21, 25, 28
International Cricket Council (ICC) 5, 28

limited overs 4, 12, 16, 27

overs 4, 6, 9, 12–13, 15–16, 19–20, 27–28

Plunket Shield 6
powerplays 13
protective clothing 5

Quaid-i-Azam Trophy 6

Ranji Trophy 7
records 5, 11, 13, 27–28
Rose bowl series 27

salaries 18
Sheffield Shield 10
Sunfoil Series 10–11

teams
    Australia 10, 12–17, 19–29

    Bangladesh 14, 17, 20–21, 28–29
    Canada 14
    Canterbury Wizards 6
    England 6, 12, 15, 16, 19–24, 26–29
    Highveld Lions 11
    India 14, 18, 21, 24–26, 28–29
    Ireland 14, 16, 26
    Kenya 6, 14, 16
    Lancashire 8–9
    Mumbai 7
    Netherlands 13–14, 16, 20, 26
    New Zealand 14–15, 17, 19, 27–29
    Northern Knights 6
    Nottinghamshire 9
    Otago Volts 6
    Pakistan 4, 8, 14, 17, 20, 28–29
    Queensland Bulls 10
    Rajasthan Royals 7, 19, 28
    Royal Challengers 18–19
    Somerset 8–9
    South Africa 5, 8, 13, 15, 17, 19–20, 24–25, 28–29
    Sri Lanka 13–17, 21, 25, 28–29
    Surrey 28
    United Arab Emirates (UAE) 14, 16
    Warwickshire 7–8, 28
    West Indies 14, 16–17, 19, 24–25, 27–29
    Yorkshire 9
Test cricket 12–14, 16, 20–26, 28
The Ashes 22–23, 26, 28–29
Triangular tournament 13
World Twenty20 16–18, 27–28

wicket-keeper 5, 7
wickets 4, 8–9, 13–15, 17, 21, 23–25
women's cricket 5, 20, 26–28
women's Cricket World Cup 26–28
World Twenty20 16–18, 27–28